EXPLORATION
of

What is Africa?

frica has always held a strong fascination for those living outside its boundaries. For people of the past, Africa represented mystery, adventure, and even danger. Yet as more of Africa was opened up, that sense of wonder only increased. The explorers returned with tales that were as fantastic as the myths that had previously surrounded this continent. Africa today remains a land of huge contrasts. To talk about something being "African" is difficult because of all the differences that do exist within its boundaries, in particular its people, and the land on which they live. It is thanks to the explorers of Africa that these wonders were first revealed to the rest of the world.

THE WILDLIFE OF AFRICA

Africa has a vast number of animal species. Its rain forests contain primates such as gorillas, monkeys, and chimpanzees. The savannahs of eastern and southern Africa have large herds of wildebeest, elephants, and zebras. The inland waters are home to the hippopotamus, crocodile, and huge flocks of birds.

LIVING ON THE EDGES OF AFRICA

The diversity of Africa's population increased with the arrival of new immigrants who originally came from Europe, South Asia, and Arabia, like this Tunisian shepherd boy.

MOUNT KILIMANJARO

Mount Kilimanjaro in Tanzania is Africa's highest mountain, rising to 19,340 feet. The first Europeans to reach Mount Kilimanjaro were two Germans, Johannes Rebmann and Ludwig Krapf, whose tales of a snow-covered mountain near the equator were not at first believed.

AFRICAN COUNTRIES

There are 51 countries in Africa. They vary widely in size and population. There are over 117 million Nigerians (about half the population of the U.S.A.), and yet the tiny republic of Sao Tome and Principe has only about 120,000 people.

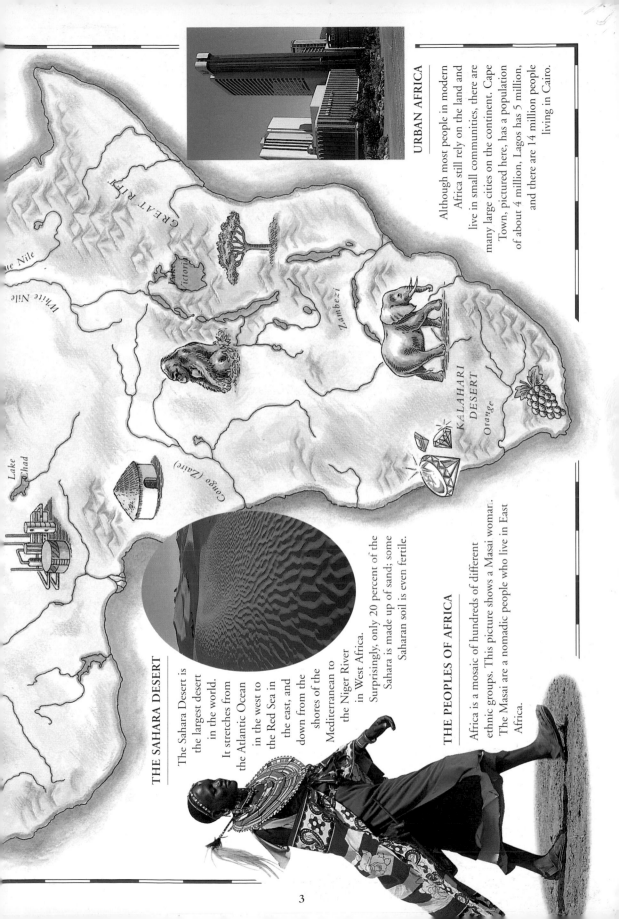

URBAN AFRICA

Although most people in modern Africa still rely on the land and live in small communities, there are many large cities on the continent. Cape Town, pictured here, has a population of about 4 million, Lagos has 5 million, and there are 14 million people living in Cairo.

THE SAHARA DESERT

The Sahara Desert is the largest desert in the world. It stretches from the Atlantic Ocean in the west to the Red Sea in the east, and down from the Mediterranean to the Niger River in West Africa.

Surprisingly, only 20 percent of the Sahara is made up of sand; some Saharan soil is even fertile.

THE PEOPLES OF AFRICA

Africa is a mosaic of hundreds of different ethnic groups. This picture shows a Masai woman. The Masai are a nomadic people who live in East Africa.

Blue Nile

White Nile

Lake Chad

Congo (Zaire)

GREAT RIFT

Lake Victoria

Zambezi

KALAHARI DESERT

Orange

MEDITERRANEAN SEA

EGYPT

Nile

RED SEA

White Nile

Blue Nile

ETHIOPIAN HIGHLANDS

— Probable route of the Egyptian expedition to Punt

Early Explorers of Africa

The exploration of Africa really began between 2,000 and 4,000 years ago. The northern coast of Africa was home to two great civilizations before the arrival of the Romans: the Phoenicians and the ancient Egyptians. Ancient Egypt developed about 5,000 years ago. The Nile River was the life blood of ancient Egypt. It flooded every year and covered the land with a fertile soil that allowed them to grow crops. The Nile also linked Egypt with the interior of Africa, but travel was difficult because the Nile was impassable in places, and the terrain east and west was inhospitable to travelers. The Egyptians needed to find alternative routes, so the Pharaoh Sahure began to send ships along the East African coast in about 2500 B.C. It was during the reign of Queen Hatshepsut, nearly 1,000 years later, that the most important ancient Egyptian voyage along the African coastline to the land known as Punt took place.

QUEEN HATSHEPSUT

This sculpture might look unusual because it shows Hatshepsut with a beard. After she became Queen of Egypt in 1489 B.C. she dressed as a king and wore a false beard. She is famous as the first woman in history whose name was actually recorded. She ordered the expedition to the land of Punt, far to the south of Egypt.

ARRIVAL AT PUNT

One of the main reasons for the Egyptian expedition to Punt was to bring back myrrh trees. Myrrh is used to produce incense which was used in religious rituals. The location of Punt is not clear, but as myrrh trees only grew in the area around modern-day Ethiopia and Somalia, most people now believe that they landed in Somalia. They returned to Egypt laden, not just with myrrh, but with ivory, ebony, and slaves.

THE ROMANS ARRIVE IN NORTH AFRICA

The great civilization of ancient Egypt began to decline in the years leading up to the birth of Christ. Much of northern Africa was conquered by the Romans by around 150 B.C. and Egypt came under their control in 30 B.C. This amphitheater at El Djem in Tunisia is the third largest amphitheater in the Roman world. It was built in A.D. 230 and could hold 50,000 spectators. The Romans rarely explored the continent but a Roman expedition is said to have reached the Tibesti highlands in modern Chad and Libya.

QUEEN HATSHEPSUT'S TEMPLE

We know a lot about the Egyptian expedition to Punt because Queen Hatshepsut had the story of the voyage carved onto the walls of her burial temple, built near Thebes at Deir el Bahri. Many objects made from the raw materials brought back from Punt were put into this temple. We do not know when Queen Hatshepsut died.

SAILING THE RED SEA

Egyptian sailing boats were made by tying planks of wood together with rope. When rope gets wet it shrinks and this made sure that the planks were always tightly held together. For the voyage to Punt, the sails would have been made larger than usual so that they could use the south wind that blows down from the Mediterranean. Each ship was about 69 feet long with a crew of 30. Five ships set off on the voyage down to the Red Sea. They supposedly sailed close to the coast and the crew always spent the night ashore, but some historians now believe that these ships were not capable of such a sea voyage and that they came down the Nile.

SETTING OFF FROM CARTHAGE

These ruins are all that remain of the great city-state of Carthage. The most famous of the Phoenician voyages was made from here by the admiral Hanno in about 425 B.C. He set sail with 60 ships; on board were hundreds of men and women. During the first part of the voyage he founded six colonies along the Moroccan coast. Hanno then continued to sail south with just two ships. He probably sailed up part of the Senegal River and then continued as far as Nigeria before returning home.

THE GREATEST MUSLIM VOYAGER

In 1325 a young man from Tangier in Morocco set off for Mecca in Arabia. His name was Ibn Battuta. On the way to Mecca he decided to travel over all of the known Muslim world and so a great journey that took him nearly 30 years began. It is known that in this time he visited Spain, the Middle East, China, India, and Southeast Asia. He also explored the north of Africa, crossed the Sahara Desert to the Niger River in West Africa, and traveled as far as modern-day Tanzania on the East African coast.

SAILING ON A PHOENICIAN SHIP

The Phoenicians were excellent ship builders, building both warships (as on this coin) and a type of sailing ship known as a Hippoi. It had a single sail, two rows of oars on either side of the ship, and a pointed bow that was used to ram enemy ships in battle. The ship was steered with two large oars at the back on cither side.

A PAPAL COMMISSION

Until Europeans began to explore the interior of Africa in the 18th century, most of their ideas about Africa came from one source. It was a book called *The Description of Africa* by Leo Africanus, which was published in 1526. Leo Africanus was born in 1485 in Granada in what is now Spain, but was then a Muslim state. In 1492 the Muslims were finally forced out of Spain and he went to live in Morocco. He worked as a diplomat in North Africa and the kingdom of Ghana before he was captured by Christian pirates. He was given to Pope Leo X (left) as a slave. Leo freed him and commissioned him to write his detailed survey of Africa.

Early Explorers of Africa

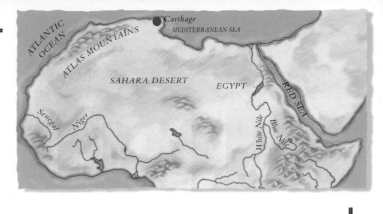

After the Egyptians, the next great explorers of Africa were the Phoenicians. These were a people who originally came from an area known as Canaan in modern-day Syria and Lebanon. They became great traders and by 1100 B.C. they were the masters of the Mediterranean. They are known to have sailed to the Atlantic and visited England in 450 B.C. Their most important exports were timber, especially cedar wood, and a purple dye made from shellfish. The word "Phoenicia" comes from a Greek word meaning purple.

In order to protect their trade, Phoenicians began to set up colonies in Spain, Sicily, Sardinia, and North Africa. Their most famous colony was the city of Carthage in modern-day Tunisia. With the decline of the Phoenician Empire, there are few accounts of further exploration of Africa until the arrival of the Portuguese in the 15th century.

A VOYAGE AROUND AFRICA?

According to the ancient Greek historian, Herodotus, the Egyptian pharaoh Necho II hired a crew of Phoenicians in 600 B.C. to sail right around the coast of Africa. Herodotus wrote that it took the crew three years to make the journey. Every spring they landed and planted grain. Only after the grain had been harvested did they continue with their voyage. We do not know whether this story is true as there is no other supporting evidence.

BUILDING FORTS ALONG THE COAST

The Portuguese were not interested in the interior of Africa. The whole continent was simply an obstacle on the way to the riches of Asia. However, they did build a series of fortified towns along the African coast to protect and supply their ships. The picture shows Fort Jesus in the Kenyan town of Mombasa.

The Portuguese in Africa

In 1492 Christopher Columbus managed to convince the Spanish monarchs, Ferdinand and Isabella, to pay for a voyage across the Atlantic. He wanted a westward route to the riches of Asia, while Portugal was looking eastward. The Portuguese had been sailing along the coast of West Africa for some time. By 1419 they had reached Madeira and in 1431 they discovered the Azores. In 1445 Portuguese ships sailed around Cape Verde. By 1482 they crossed the equator and had sailed as far south as the mouth of the Congo River. When the Spanish discovered a "New World" to the west it was believed they had reached the Asian continent, rather than America. This made the Portuguese search for their own route around Africa more urgent.

MEETINGS ON THE AFRICAN COAST

As the Portuguese sailed down the western coast of Africa they found that many of the peoples that they met belonged to highly developed societies. This bronze model of a Portuguese soldier was made by a member of the Benin empire. The people of Benin lived in what is now Nigeria.

8

PRINCE HENRY THE NAVIGATOR

Prince Henry directed the early Portuguese exploration of West Africa. He dreamed of launching a crusade to destroy Muslim North Africa. Finding a way to Asia would help to pay for this crusade and at the same time would weaken the hold that the Muslims had over the trade in gold and spices between Europe and Asia.

MARKED WITH A CROSS

Among the supplies that Vasco da Gama carried on his voyage were stone crosses called padroes. These were set in high ground as markers for the sailors who were to follow them. They were also used to claim newly discovered lands. This cross is at Malindi in modern-day Kenya.

ROUNDING THE CAPE OF GOOD HOPE

In 1488 Bartolomeo Diaz sailed around the southern tip of Africa. Diaz had lost sight of land after a storm. When it became calm he sailed north and found that the African coast now ran from west to east, rather than north to south. He had found the southern tip of Africa almost by accident. Diaz called this point "Cabom Tormentoso," which means the Cape of Storms. King John II of Portugal later rejected this name as too gloomy and renamed it the Cape of Good Hope.

ARRIVAL IN INDIA

It took another ten years after Bartolomeo Diaz had discovered the route around Africa for the Portuguese to eventually sail all the way to Asia. Vasco da Gama set off from Portugal in July 1497 and, guided by an East African pilot across the Indian Ocean, he finally arrived at the southern Indian port of Calicut in May 1498.

THE LEGEND OF PRESTER JOHN

The main reason why Europeans were searching for a seaward route to Asia was because the land route was controlled by hostile Muslims. There was a legend of a Christian king called Prester John who ruled over an African kingdom just beyond Muslim North Africa. Portuguese explorers hoped to find Prester John and join with him to fight the Muslims.

AFRICA
-A Time Line-

~1526~
The Description of Africa by *Leo Africanus* is first published.

~1768~
James Bruce, the Laird of Kinnaird, begins his voyage across Egypt and Ethiopia.

~1770~
James Bruce reaches Lake Tana in Ethiopia, which he mistakenly believes is the source of the Nile River.

~1771~
Mungo Park born.

~1795–1797~
Mungo Park goes in search of the source of the Niger River.

~1813~
David Livingstone born.

~1822~
Hugh Clapperton crosses the Sahara Desert to Lake Chad.

~1824–1828~
René Caillié travels through West Africa to Timbuktu.

EGYPT

SAHARA
DESERT

RED SEA

White Nile

Blue Nile

ETHIOPIAN
HIGHLANDS

Lake
Victoria

Lake
Tanganika

- Speke & Grant
- Burton & Speke
- Speke
- Baker

The Search for the Source of the Nile

The search for the source of the Nile had fascinated people for centuries. Ancient Greeks and Romans used the expression "to seek the head of the Nile" when they were describing an impossible task. It was long believed that if the source could be found then all the rest of the mysteries of the interior of Africa would be revealed. By the 19th century the need to discover the source became more than just satisfying people's curiosity. The European powers were beginning to expand their influence around the world and the Nile was recognized as an important part of that expansion.

SIR RICHARD BURTON

Sir Richard Francis Burton was an intrepid English explorer who traveled with Speke in search of the source. Apart from discovering Lake Tanganika, he is also known for visiting the Muslim holy cities of Mecca and Medina in disguise.

SIR SAMUEL WHITE BAKER

With a complicated river like the Nile there were bound to be mistaken claims by those who were looking for its origins. However, the expedition of Sir Samuel Baker did help determine where the Nile *didn't* start. In 1861 he followed the river south and discovered Lake Albert Nyanza on the border of Zaire and Uganda. He found that the Nile just flowed through the lake.

MEETING OF THE NILE EXPLORERS

The picture shows Speke and Grant meeting up with Sir Samuel Baker in 1863. The other person at the table is Samuel Baker's wife, Florence. At a time when women were not expected to do anything even mildly adventurous, she traveled with her husband during all of his expeditions. She had married Samuel Baker after being bought by him at a slave market in Bulgaria.

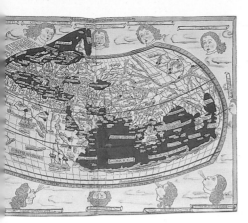

ANCIENT VIEW OF THE NILE

This picture is known as Ptolemy's world map, although it was actually drawn in 1482, more than 1,000 years after his death. The Nile is shown coming from a series of lakes far to the south of the equator. Just below these lakes is a mountain range called the Mountains of the Moon.

FALLS ON THE BLUE NILE

The Nile is the longest river in the world at about 4,160 miles long. There are several tributaries that also feed the main river. These include the Blue Nile, which starts in the highlands of Ethiopia, and the smaller tributaries in Burundi, Kenya, and Tanzania. About 1,863 miles of the Nile are navigable.

JAMES BRUCE

Scottish aristocrat, James Bruce, Laird of Kinnaird, set off in 1768 and traveled across Egypt and Ethiopia in search of the source of the Nile. In 1770 he reached Lake Tana in Ethiopia, which he mistakenly believed was the source. He had found the source of the Blue Nile, a tributary of the main river, and was not the first – a Spanish missionary had reached Lake Tana over 150 years before.

THE SOURCE DISCOVERED

It was the British explorer John Hanning Speke who found the true source of the Nile. In 1856 Speke and Sir Richard Burton went to search for great lakes in East Africa. In 1858 they found Lake Tanganyika. Speke traveled on alone after Burton fell ill, and discovered Lake Victoria, which he believed was the source of the Nile. Lake Victoria lies within Uganda, Tanzania, and Kenya. He returned there with James Grant in 1862 and found the point at which the Nile flowed out of the lake.

MOUNT KENYA

Mount Kenya is an extinct volcano in central Kenya. It is 17,058 feet high and is Africa's second highest mountain. The summit was first reached in 1899 by a party led by the British geographer Sir Halford Mackinder.

AFRICA'S GREAT RIFT

The Ngorongoro Crater in Tanzania is just one of the remarkable features of Africa's Great Rift. A series of faults in the Earth have created a region cutting from the Red Sea down to Mozambique that is made up of mountains, volcanoes, valleys, and deep lakes. A branch in the east is named after John Gregory, a British explorer and geologist who explored the region in 1893.

GUSTAV NACHTIGAL

Gustav Nachtigal was a German explorer who in 1868 was sent by the king of Prussia on a mission to Kanem-Bornu, a powerful kingdom situated in the Lake Chad region. He was the first European to travel through areas of the central Sahara in what is now Chad and the Sudan. He arrived back in Cairo in 1874.

Exploring East Africa

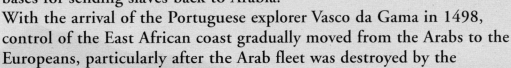

From the 7th century onwards, East Africa increasingly came under the influence of Arab traders from the Middle East. The Arabs built many towns and ports along the coast that were used as centers for trading and as bases for sending slaves back to Arabia. With the arrival of the Portuguese explorer Vasco da Gama in 1498, control of the East African coast gradually moved from the Arabs to the Europeans, particularly after the Arab fleet was destroyed by the Portuguese at the battle of Diu in 1509. Any country that wanted to dominate trade with Asia, particularly India, had to be in control of the East African coast. By the end of the 19th century this meant that the interior of East Africa was explored, mapped, and claimed on behalf of various European countries. As the power of Portugal declined, it was the British and the newly created countries of Germany and Italy that increasingly took charge of East Africa.

JOSEPH THOMSON

Joseph Thomson was a Scottish explorer who traveled over much of eastern and southern Africa. He studied geology at the University of Edinburgh before leading an expedition to Lakes Tanganyika and Rukwa in 1879–80. Four years later, he became the first European to cross modern Kenya.

LAKE TANGANYIKA

Lake Tanganyika is located along the Rift Valley. It is the second largest lake in Africa and the second deepest lake in the world. It is bounded by Tanzania, Zaire, Burundi, and Zambia. The first Europeans to reach Lake Tanganyika were John Hanning Speke and Sir Richard Burton in February 1858. At first they thought they had found the source of the Nile.

AFRICA
-A Time Line-

~1830~
*Richard and John Lander
find the source of
the Niger.*

~1835~
*The Boers begin the
Great Trek.*

~1841~
Henry Stanley born.

~1848~
*Johannes Rebmann and
Ludwig Krapf discover Mount
Kilimanjaro.*

~1849–1852 ~
*Livingstone's first exploration
of Africa's interior.*

~1852–1856~
Livingstone's second voyage.

~1855~
*Livingstone sees Victoria Falls
for the first time.*

~1856~
*John Hanning Speke and
Sir Richard Burton begin
their search for the source
of the Nile.*

~1858~
*Lake Tanganyika discovered by
Speke and Burton.*

A ROMANTIC EXPLORER

René Caillié was inspired to explore Africa after reading Daniel Defoe's *Robinson Crusoe.* He took up a challenge from the French Geographical Society to reach Timbuktu and return with an account of his journey. Caillié started his journey in Sierra Leone, disguised himself as an Arab, and joined a trade caravan heading for Timbuktu. Remarkably, the fact that he could not speak Arabic and knew nothing of the Muslim faith aroused little suspicion. He eventually arrived home to a hero's welcome.

CONTACT WITH WEST AFRICANS

All of these explorers met a wide variety of different people in their travels. In West Africa the main societies were the Mande and Akan groups who lived in Ghana and the Ivory Coast. The Fulani, Hausa, and Yoruba peoples lived around what is now Nigeria. There are many other groups throughout the whole of West Africa. The Ivory Coast, where this mask comes from, has over 60 ethnic groups within its borders.

MUNGO PARK

Mungo Park was born in Scotland in 1771 and trained to be a surgeon. He led an expedition to the Niger River, and after landing in what is now The Gambia, he traveled inland, going further eastward than any other European before him. He was captured by a local tribe and was a prisoner for four months before escaping. He reached the Niger in 1796 and turned back only when his supplies ran out. He returned nine years later to explore the Niger by canoe, but this time his expedition was attacked by local people and he was drowned.

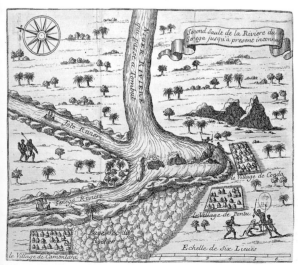

Exploring West Africa

Much of the West African coast was very well known to Europeans by the 19th century. It was due to the Portuguese explorers of the 15th century that this whole area had been thoroughly mapped and charted. Until the building of the Suez Canal in 1869, the only viable way for Europeans to reach Asia was by sailing around Africa. This meant that the whole of this part of the west coast was very important since whoever controlled it could have some control of the sea route to Asia. It was also from this part of Africa that Europeans took slaves to work on their plantations in the Caribbean and America. By the end of the 19th century it was the British and the French who controlled the coastline; and explorers of both countries began to travel into the interior of West Africa.

MEETING THE HAUSA

In 1822 the Scottish explorer Hugh Clapperton crossed the Sahara Desert to Lake Chad. He then went on to become the first European to come into contact with the Hausa people of northern Nigeria. After a short trip home he returned to find where the Niger River flowed into the sea. He died near Sokoto in April 1827 without achieving his goal.

FRANCE CLAIMS THE CONGO

The most famous French explorer of Africa, Pierre De Brazza, was an Italian aristocrat by birth who took French citizenship. He explored West Africa for six years in the 1870s and 1880s. As the picture shows, De Brazza convinced many African leaders to accept French influence in the area.

FROM EAST TO WEST

The English explorer Verney Lovett Cameron was the first European to cross Africa from east to west. In 1873 he led an expedition to search for the explorer David Livingstone. Finding him dead, Cameron went on to the Zambezi and Congo Rivers. Here he is shown being received by a king of the Congo region.

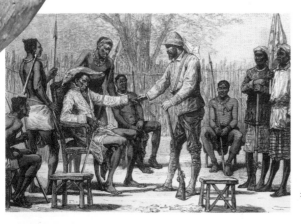

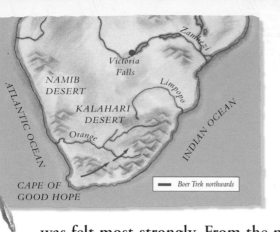

Exploring Southern Africa

Of all the parts of Africa with which Europeans came into contact, it was southern Africa where their presence was felt most strongly. From the moment Bartolomeo Diaz accidentally sailed around the Cape of Good Hope in 1488, the strategic importance of this whole region was instantly recognized by every sea-faring European power. The Portuguese had not been interested in colonizing southern Africa, so it was the Dutch who were the first to settle there in the middle of the 17th century. They became known as Boers, which comes from the Dutch word for "farmer." By the 19th century other European colonists began to arrive, especially from Britain. Tension began to arise between these different groups and as a result Boers moved further into the unexplored areas of South Africa.

THE DUTCH EAST INDIA COMPANY

The Dutch East India Company was established to conduct Eastern trade, and in turn created a Dutch empire in Southeast Asia in the 17th and 18th centuries. It controlled all commerce between the Dutch Republic and the East.

A COLONY ON THE CAPE

The Dutch settled at Table Bay to grow vegetables for passing ships, to build a hospital for sailors, and to repair ships. Jan van Riebeeck's first fort was modern-day Cape Town's first building. It was to become the first town founded by Europeans in southern Africa.

THE DUTCH COLONY BEGINS

In 1652 the Dutch East India Company gave in to repeated petitions and recommendations from their ships' officers and decided to establish a post at Table Bay at the bottom of Table Mountain. They sent three small ships, the *Dromedaris*, the *Reijger*, and the *Goede Hoop* under the command of 23-year-old Jan Antony van Riebeeck, a ship's surgeon, to establish a stronghold on the shores of Table Bay.

LES BOERS

3. — Combat avec les Matabélé à Wilge-River.

THE GREAT TREK

From 1835 until 1843 the Boers began an epic journey that became known as the Great Trek. Over 14,000 people left Cape Colony and moved inland to set up new colonies in Natal, the Orange Free State, and the Transvaal. The Great Trek took place for two reasons – the Boers were looking for new pastures for their cattle, and they were unhappy with British control of Cape Colony, especially after the British abolished slavery in 1833. During the Great Trek the Boers came into conflict with native Africans, especially the Matabele and Zulus, who did not want these new arrivals on their land.

AFRICAN RESISTANCE

It was not only the Dutch who had to fight Africans before laying claim to African lands. In the 1870s the Zulu chief Cetewayo asked the British authorities to protect his lands from the Boers. The British responded by invading Zululand in 1879. Cetewayo defeated the British at Isandhlwana before finally being crushed.

GREAT ZIMBABWE

As the Boers moved into new areas, they believed that they were settling in areas where no civilization had existed before. The complex of ruins of Great Zimbabwe covers nearly 2,000 acres. It is said to have been built by Shona people in the 13th or 14th centuries. It may have housed as many as 40,000. The first Europeans to see it were unwilling to believe that it was built by Africans because there was nothing else like it in all of southern Africa.

ARRIVING AT THE CAPE

Cape Colony had originally been colonized by the Boers like the ones shown in this picture. When Livingstone arrived in March 1841, Cape Colony was under British control. He moved north and started his missionary work. By 1849 the urge to travel was too strong and Livingstone joined an expedition to cross the Kalahari Desert. They became the first Europeans to reach Lake Ngami in modern-day Angola. When Livingstone returned to his home he wrote to London announcing the news of their discoveries.

WORKING AT THE MILL

Livingstone started work at a cotton mill next to his house when he was ten years old. He read constantly and soon decided to become a doctor. In 1836 he managed to get to medical school in Glasgow. While he was there he became interested in the work of the London Missionary Society and he decided to do missionary work in China. The Society accepted Livingstone but sent him to southern Africa instead.

GROWING UP IN GLASGOW

David Livingstone was born in 1813 and was brought up on the edge of Glasgow. He shared a single room with his parents, two brothers, and two sisters. The room was about 15 square feet. Although this seems small now, at the time it was regarded as being quite comfortable.

FROM SOLDIER TO JOURNALIST

In 1862 Henry Stanley joined the army. He soon found himself fighting in the American Civil War on the side of the Confederates, who were to later lose the war. Stanley was wounded in his first battle and taken prisoner. After he recovered he became a sailor and later a journalist. He worked for the *New York Herald* in Europe and Africa, and in 1871 he was sent to find Livingstone.

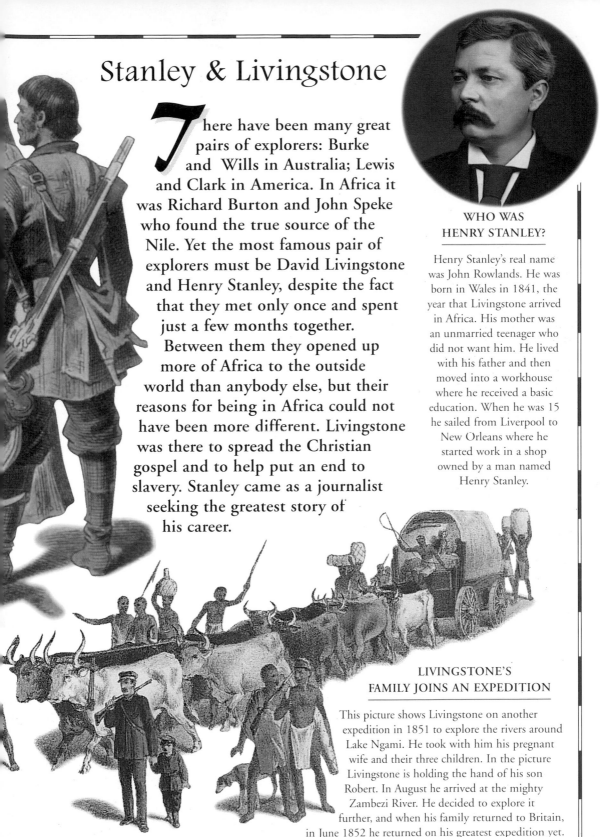

Stanley & Livingstone

*T*here have been many great pairs of explorers: Burke and Wills in Australia; Lewis and Clark in America. In Africa it was Richard Burton and John Speke who found the true source of the Nile. Yet the most famous pair of explorers must be David Livingstone and Henry Stanley, despite the fact that they met only once and spent just a few months together.

Between them they opened up more of Africa to the outside world than anybody else, but their reasons for being in Africa could not have been more different. Livingstone was there to spread the Christian gospel and to help put an end to slavery. Stanley came as a journalist seeking the greatest story of his career.

WHO WAS HENRY STANLEY?

Henry Stanley's real name was John Rowlands. He was born in Wales in 1841, the year that Livingstone arrived in Africa. His mother was an unmarried teenager who did not want him. He lived with his father and then moved into a workhouse where he received a basic education. When he was 15 he sailed from Liverpool to New Orleans where he started work in a shop owned by a man named Henry Stanley.

LIVINGSTONE'S FAMILY JOINS AN EXPEDITION

This picture shows Livingstone on another expedition in 1851 to explore the rivers around Lake Ngami. He took with him his pregnant wife and their three children. In the picture Livingstone is holding the hand of his son Robert. In August he arrived at the mighty Zambezi River. He decided to explore it further, and when his family returned to Britain, in June 1852 he returned on his greatest expedition yet.

Stanley & Livingstone

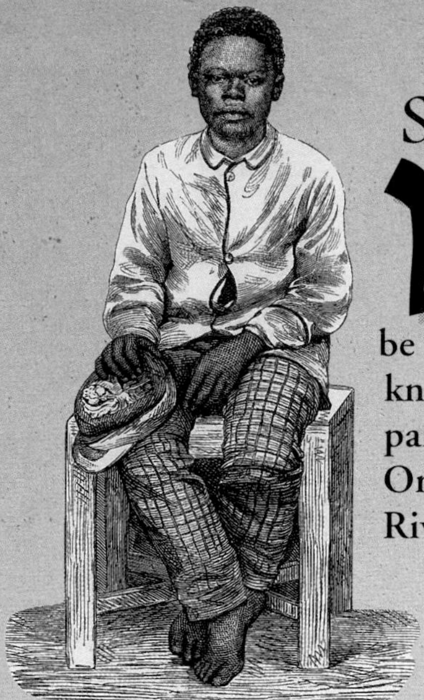

When Livingstone set off on his second expedition in June 1852, he had little idea that he would not be seeing his family for four years. He did not know that he would travel almost 5,600 miles through parts of Africa that had never been seen by any European. On this expedition he explored more of the Zambezi River and was the first white person ever to see the Victoria Falls. When he returned to Britain he was a national hero and easily found the money for his next two expeditions, in 1858 and 1866. During this last expedition Livingstone was away for so long that most people in Britain assumed that he was dead. The *New York Herald* sent Stanley to discover if this was true, and their meeting is now one of the most famous in history. After five months Stanley returned to Europe to tell an expectant public of his adventures. Livingstone remained in Africa and died there in May 1873.

THE DEATH OF LIVINGSTONE

When Stanley left Livingstone in March 1872 he left behind a sick and weak man. But Livingstone continued with his travels for another eight months until he died on May 1, 1873. His African companions, including his servant Chuma pictured here, preserved his body and carried it over 1,200 miles to the coast. Livingstone was buried at Westminster Abbey and mourned as a national hero.

VICTORIA FALLS

From 1852 to 1855 Livingstone had been following the Zambezi River downstream. Frequent illness and low supplies often slowed the expedition down. However, on November 16, 1855, Livingstone saw the Victoria Falls. The local name for the Falls was "Mosi-oa-Tunya" which meant "smoke that thunders." Livingstone decided to rename it after the British queen.

FIGHTING THE SLAVE TRADE

One of the main reasons that Livingstone returned to Africa was to fight the slave trade. His determination to rid Africa of this evil was strengthened in July 1871 when he witnessed a massacre of over 400 Africans by Arab slavers. It was Stanley who brought back news of this massacre and the strength of public opinion forced the British government to take action against the slavers. Ironically, Stanley became notorious for treating his African porters harshly. He put them in chains to stop them from running away and many died accompanying him.

STANLEY AND LIVINGSTONE MEET

Led by an African carrying the American flag Stanley traveled almost 500 miles inland from the East African coast. As Stanley approached Ujiji on the shores of Lake Tanganyika he was told that a white man was staying there. Stanley changed into his cleanest clothes and walked into Ujiji. He stepped up to Livingstone and said *"Doctor Livingstone, I Presume?"*

Essential Equipment for African Explorers

Whenever European explorers arrived in Africa they were stepping into the unknown. Explorers had to travel across the variety of landscapes that is Africa. They could find themselves in a seemingly empty desert, a foul-smelling swamp, or thick rainforest. Even with African guides they did not know what dangers and obstacles they would have to face. To overcome these problems, and since these expeditions sometimes took several years, explorers had to take several tons of equipment. Carrying all of this, and sharing the dangers, were native porters who followed the expedition.

CARRYING A GUN

Two of the dangers that were faced by explorers were attacks either by wildlife or by native people who thought they might be slavers. Therefore, a gun was a useful tool for both dangers. Stanley often made use of the elephant gun he is carrying in this picture. The explosive bullet was powerful enough to destroy a small boat. Although most animals kept clear of teams of explorers, Livingstone himself was once attacked by a lion.

USING A COMPASS AND SEXTANT

Since much of the exploration of the interior of Africa was done by river, it may not be surprising that explorers used the same kind of navigational equipment used by sailors. This compass and sextant were used by Livingstone during his travels along the Zambezi River. The compass was used to discover the direction in which the explorers were going. The sextant measured the angles between two stars and the horizon to establish their longitude.

THE MENACE OF THE MOSQUITO

The greatest menace faced by any African explorer was the often fatal disease of malaria, which in 1888 was discovered to be transmitted by mosquito bites. However, the explorers did know that quinine could prevent malaria and many of them took some on their expeditions.

CARRYING THE EQUIPMENT

When traveling by land explorers depended on African porters to carry their equipment. Neither Livingstone nor Stanley traveled with less than 20 African porters and most explorers had over 50. These men and women would carry loads of around 100 pounds, day after day.

EXPLORERS' CLOTHING

European explorers did not even dream of wearing the same clothes as their African porters, and many of them wore clothes that were similar to what they might wear at home. One exception was the pith helmet which was developed by the British army in India. It was made from compressed plant fibers and had a deep brim. Some helmets had ventilation holes that helped to keep the head cool.

CROSSING WATERFALLS

When explorers came up against such barriers as rapids and waterfalls they had no choice but to carry the boat around the obstacle. This picture shows porters carrying dugout canoes alongside the Congo River.

AFRICA
-A Time Line-

~1858~
Speke finds the source of the Nile, Lake Victoria.

~1858–1864~
Livingstone explores the Zambezi River.

~1860–1863~
Speke returns to Lake Victoria with James Grant.

~1861~
Sir Samuel and Florence Baker follow the Nile south and discover Lake Albert Nyanza.

~1866–1873~
Livingstone's last voyage.

~1868–1874~
Gustav Nachtigal becomes the first European to travel through the central Sahara Desert.

~1873~
David Livingstone dies.

~1873–1875~
Verney Lovett Cameron is the first European to cross Africa from east to west.

~1874–1877~
Henry Stanley explores the Congo River.

CARL THUNBERG

It was because of two men that the wonders of Africa's living world were brought to international attention. They were the Swedes Carl Thunberg (pictured here) and Anders Sparrman. In 1722 they traveled to the Cape of Good Hope. On arrival they headed for Table Mountain and in the space of one day managed to collect over 300 plant specimens, many of which they had never seen before.

PROVIDING MEDICINE

Because they had lived in Africa for thousands of years many Africans had developed a natural resistance to many diseases such as malaria. However, this resistance did not offer complete protection and there were many other diseases such as yellow fever or cholera to which Africans had no natural resistance. The ability to immunize against some of these diseases by vaccination was a practice started in England in 1796. This picture shows European doctors giving vaccinations to African children. Stanley made sure that all of his porters were given quinine, which helps protect against malaria.

ANIMALS AS TROPHIES

Hunting has always been a central feature in the lives of many Africans. It was essential for survival, and even the first European settlers hunted for food. The Boers were responsible for the extinction of the quagga, a kind of zebra. For later settlers, hunting for food was less important than hunting for sport. The most popular hunting areas in the 19th century were Kenya in East Africa and Zambia in southern Africa.

DRAWING THE WILDLIFE

Today most people hunt African animals with cameras rather than guns, but in the last century cameras were rare and naturalists could only shoot or draw the animals that they saw. Many of the naturalists who came to Africa, like William Paterson or Cornwallis Harris, were also talented artists.

Their drawings and watercolors beautifully capture the colorful variety of Africa's natural world.

Following the Explorers ~ Science & Recreation

The flora and fauna of Africa remained a mystery for centuries. It was believed that the bones of lions were as hard as flint and created sparks when struck together. It was said that a rhinoceros killed its prey by knocking it down and licking it to death. Elephants always stirred the water with their trunks before drinking because they could not bear to see their own reflections. Yet, as with so much of Africa, the truth managed to be even more unusual than even these stories. Naturalists and scientists who came to Africa were amazed by the variety of wildlife that they encountered and they hurried to take specimens home. William Burchell, an English naturalist, returned from South Africa with thousands of specimens including 265 bird skins and over 120 animal skins. There were other Europeans who were interested in the animals of Africa. They were not scientists but hunters who entertained themselves by shooting the wildlife.

PLANT-HUNTING

Many of the naturalists who came to Africa were not interested in the animal world. Cape Colony in South Africa was a treasure trove for all botanists. There were plants that attracted insects with the odor of rotting flesh and others that flowered only at night. The picture above shows the *Protea*, the national flower of modern South Africa.

A WOMAN IN AFRICA

At a time when women were not expected to look much further than their homes, Africa lured some exceptional women explorers. Perhaps the most famous is Mary Kingsley who, interested in new animals species, explored much of West Africa. She lived with native people there, and was the first European to visit parts of Gabon in 1894.

SPREADING THE WORD

In several European countries and in North America missionary societies were formed in order to try to convert Africans to Christianity. David Livingstone was sent to Africa by the London Missionary Society. Most of these societies worked with little money and they had to rely on missionaries who traveled around in tents.

A SCOTTISH MISSIONARY

One of the best-known missionaries in Africa was Robert Moffat. He was sent to South Africa by the London Missionary Society in 1816 and he stayed for over 50 years. He encouraged Livingstone to explore Africa and later Livingstone married his daughter, Mary.

Following the Explorers ~ Religion & Economics

Many of the Europeans who followed in the footsteps of the explorers were not interested in discovering new lands and new peoples. In the 19th century it was sincerely believed that the European or American way of life was superior to anything else that existed at that time. When some Europeans looked at Africa they saw a continent that appeared to be empty of agriculture and industry. Others were concerned with changing the people of Africa who they saw as primitive and superstitious. They believed that if these people could be converted to Christianity, then Africa would become more "civilized." So many Europeans came to Africa in order to develop this undeveloped continent. Some of these new arrivals saw opportunities for themselves but all felt it necessary to impose their ways and beliefs on those they saw as inferior.

INTRODUCING CROPS

European farmers began to introduce crops into Africa that were more profitable than native plants. Many of these new plants, such as the peanut, sweet potato, or the cocoa bean as shown here, originally came from the Americas. These crops are still important to many modern African countries.

BUILDING AN AFRICAN CHURCH

Today there are about 160 million Christians in Africa. They are roughly divided between the Roman Catholic Church and the various Protestant churches. Africa is home to the largest church in the world. The Basilica of Our Lady of Peace in Yamoussoukro in the Ivory Coast was completed in 1989. It has a total area of over 107,000 square yards and can seat 7,000.

THE CHALLENGE OF ISLAM

The Islamic faith had already made many converts in Africa. When Islam spread across North Africa in the 7th and 8th centuries it also spread southwards to those areas that bordered the Sahara Desert. The East African coast had been dominated by Arab traders for centuries and the Muslim faith was very strongly rooted.

LOOKING FOR PRECIOUS STONES

In February 1867 a 15-year-old Boer, Erasmus Jacobs, found a shining stone on the bank of the Orange River. It was a diamond. Within 15 years, South Africa was producing more diamonds than any other part of the world.

INTRODUCING AGRICULTURE

For centuries Africans practiced a form of agriculture called slash-and-burn. A small area of forest was cut down and burned. The area was then farmed until it was no longer fertile and then abandoned. It was then gradually reclaimed by the forest. This method of farming began to vanish with the arrival of European farming methods.

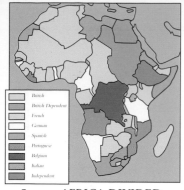

The Carving-up of Africa

19th-century Europe was changing fast. Nations that once depended on agriculture for their wealth now relied on industry and manufacturing. In order to grow more prosperous, Europeans searched for new ways to sell more of their produce and find cheap raw materials to make their goods. Explorers had shown that the interior of Africa was, more than likely, rich in resources to be exploited. The European countries made sure that they could control the African market by taking over large areas of the continent. During the 19th century Europe saw the creation of three new countries, Belgium, Italy, and Germany. These three countries looked to Africa as a way of proving that they were equal to any of the older nations like France and Britain. As Africa was "carved-up" by these European powers nobody stopped to wonder what the people of Africa actually wanted for themselves.

AFRICA DIVIDED

This map shows how the European nations divided up Africa among them. Belgium kept the Congo. France had most of West Africa. Britain had a large share including most of southern Africa. Germany, Portugal, and Spain also took chunks of land. By the end of the 19th century there were only two independent African nations, Liberia and Abyssinia, which is now Ethiopia.

THE BERLIN CONFERENCE

King Leopold's actions in the Congo prompted other European powers to lay claim to much of the rest of Africa. Sometimes these claims were a source of argument between the various nations. In 1884 a conference of European nations was held in Berlin to sort these disputes out, and Africa was formally divided. In this picture an African looks on helplessly as his destiny is decided by European leaders.

AFRICAN RESISTANCE

Many Africans did not want their lands to be ruled by Europeans and resistance was widespread. However, they could do little against heavily armed and disciplined armies and hundreds of thousands of Africans died. One of the most formidable opponents the British had to face were the Zulus who were finally defeated in 1879.

RHODES: THE EMPIRE BUILDER

Cecil John Rhodes was a British politician who did more than anybody to bring southern Africa under British rule. In 1890 he became Prime Minister of Cape Colony and used his power to weaken the power of the Boers. As the picture shows, he dreamed of creating an empire from the Cape to Cairo. He invaded the lands of the Shona and Ndebebe people in what was later called Rhodesia.

KING LEOPOLD OF BELGIUM

Leopold II hired Henry Stanley to carve out an empire for him in Central Africa, which he called the Congo Free State. He claimed it was to advance the cause of the abolition of slavery. By the 1880s it was clear that Leopold's real motive was to develop a rubber industry there and that Belgians were themselves acting cruelly towards the Africans in the Congo.

AFRICA
-A TIME LINE-

~1879~
The Zulu king, Cetawayo, is defeated by British forces.

~1879–1880~
Joseph Thomson explores Lakes Tanganyika and Rukwa.

~1883–1884~
Joseph Thomson becomes the first European to cross modern-day Kenya.

~1884~
The Berlin Conference is held.

~1887–1889~
Stanley's last expedition to Africa.

~1893~
Mary Kingsley explores parts of the Congo.

~1894–1895~
Modern-day Gabon is explored by Mary Kingsley.

~1899~
Mount Kenya is successfully climbed by Sir Halford Mackinder.

~1904~
Stanley dies.

THE BOER WAR

When gold was discovered in South Africa in 1884, thousands of British settlers came to make their fortune. Resentment between these newcomers and the Boers eventually turned into conflict and in 1899 the Boers declared war on Britain. It took three years for the British army to finally defeat them.

Africa Today

A SYMBOL OF PRIDE

In 1965 the white ruling classes of Rhodesia declared themselves independent of Britain rather than allow democracy. African resistance to this was led by Robert Mugabe and Joshua Nkomo. In March 1980 additional international pressure forced the Rhodesian government to hold elections. Mugabe's ZANU-PF party won and Rhodesia became Zimbabwe.

In February 1960 the British Prime Minister, Harold Macmillan, gave a speech to the South African parliament in Cape Town. He spoke of a new African nationalism that was sweeping through the continent. He said, *"The wind of change is blowing through this continent and...this growth of national consciousness is a political fact."* Those winds had started blowing after the end of the Second World War. The Allies had fought to allow European and Asian countries to choose their own governments. Africans began to ask why the same should be not true for them and demands for self-rule became louder. Sometimes the Europeans handed over power without a struggle. Sometimes Africans had to fight for independence. Since the 1950s every African country has managed to become independent. However, it was only in 1994, when South Africa became a democratic country, that the continent was returned to the people to whom it had originally belonged before the explorers came.

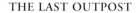

THE LAST OUTPOST

After the Second World War the South African government passed a series of laws that made the black population second-class citizens in their own land. This system of government was called "apartheid." Black South Africans struggled against this injustice both peacefully and with weapons. In 1990 Nelson Mandela, the leader of the African National Congress, was released from prison after 27 years. In April 1994 the first multi-racial elections were held and Mandela, aged 75, became president of a new South Africa.

THE FUTURE OF AFRICA

Africa has to face many of the same problems as the rest of the developing world. Every African government has the twin problems of improving the living standards of their people while coping with a growing population and increasing environmental damage. The estimated population of Africa is 763 million. By 2010 this will rise to 979 million and by 2025 it is projected to be 1,228 million. This is mostly because nearly half of all Africans alive today are, like these children in Nairobi, under 15 years of age.

CONFLICT IN AFRICA

Many of these newly independent countries had borders that had been created by the Berlin Conference. Different groups of people that had lived separately for centuries suddenly found that they now lived in the same country. This has been one of the main reasons for the civil wars that have become a way of life in several African countries today.

AFRICA WORKING TOGETHER

This picture shows Nelson Mandela being helped down from a platform by other African presidents, after addressing the Organization of African Unity in June 1998. The organization was founded in 1958 and exists to help African countries find common solutions to common problems.

THE FIRST INDEPENDENT

The first colony to become independent after the end of the Second World War was the Gold Coast in 1957. The name of the country was changed to Ghana soon after independence. Kwame Nkrumah became the first African leader of a new African country.

DID YOU KNOW?

Which country sent the most explorers to Africa? The explorers of Africa came from all over the continent of Europe. However, it was the small country of Scotland that produced more explorers than any other. The list of Scottish explorers includes Mungo Park, David Livingstone, Joseph Thomson, Hugh Clapperton, and Verney Lovett Cameron. It is difficult to find a reason why Scottish explorers outnumbered all others. It is certainly true that Scottish people traveled all over the world in the 19th century to start a new life in a new land. Many modern Americans and Australians can trace their family line back to Scotland.

How Stanley carried his boat, the _Lady Alice,_ overland? Both Livingstone and Stanley relied on boats to explore the interior of Africa. However, there were many times when they had to be carried because the river was too shallow or rocky, or there was a waterfall. Stanley made the job easier by having his boat divided into eight sections. Each section was light enough to be carried by two African porters and could easily be fastened together again.

Why Europeans were so fascinated by the African city of Timbuktu? Many of the European explorers who came to Africa did so in order to enter the Malian city of Timbuktu. Founded in the 11th century, it became a major center of Muslim learning and culture in the 15th century. One of the world's first universities was established here. Like the holy city of Mecca, it was out of bounds to nonMuslims so, for Europeans, it represented the mystery of Muslim culture. If Timbuktu could be understood, then so might the rest of the Muslim world.

Who was the first white person to see a gorilla? The American explorer, Paul de Chaillu, returned home from Africa in 1859 with the first report of a gorilla sighting by a white person. He wrote: _"Nearly six feet high, with immense body, huge chest, and great muscular arms, with fiercely glaring large deep grey eyes and a hellish expression of face, which seemed to me like some nightmare vision."_ His description did much to damage the reputation of this gentle animal and gave rise to films like _King Kong._

How diamonds are made? A diamond is a mineral that is made of pure, natural carbon. The atoms are packed closely together in cube shapes, making it the hardest substance in the world. The largest diamond was found in South Africa in 1902 and was called the Cullinan diamond. It weighed over 2 pounds (1 kilogram) and was cut up to produce several gemstones for the British crown jewels. This includes the "Star of Africa," the largest cut diamond in the world today.

ACKNOWLEDGMENTS

The publishers would like to thank: Graham Rich, Neil Grant, Jan Alvey and Elizabeth Wiggans for their assistance and David Hobbs for his map of Africa.
First edition for the United States, its territories and dependencies, Canada, and the Philippine Republic, published 1998 by Barron's Educational Series, Inc.
Original edition copyright © 1998 by ticktock Publishing, Ltd.
U.S. edition copyright © 1998 by Barron's Educational Series, Inc.

All inquiries should be addressed to:
Barron's Educational Series, Inc., 250 Wireless Boulevard, Hauppauge, New York 11788 **http://www.barronseduc.com**
Library of Congress Catalog Card No. 98-73624   International Standard Book No. 0-7641-0632-5
987654321   Printed in The United Kingdom.

Picture Credits: t=top, b=bottom, c=center, l=left, r=right, OBC=outside back cover, OFC=outside front cover, IFC=inside front cover

AKG; OFC (main pic), 4bl & OFC, 6/7c & OBC, 6bl, 10/11t, 12tr, 14/15c & 32c, 17tr, 18/19t & OBC, 20/21t, 26/27t & OFC, 26tl, 26/27b, 28c. Ann Ronan @ Image Select; 5c, 10cb, 18tl, 18bl & OBC, 19tr, 19b, 21tr, 22/23t, 23cb, 25br, 26cl, 28/29c. Ann Ronan Picture Library; 10/11b, 13cr, 15bl. Associated Press; 31c. Bridgeman Art Library; 8bl & OFC, 16br , 16/17c, 20/21 (main pic), 22cb, 22/23b, 24/25b, 27br & OFC. C.F.C.L/Image Select; 3ct, 25tl. Colourific!; 12/13 (main pic), 30bl. e.t.archive; 28bl. Fotomas; 13cl, 17br, 20tl, 23c, 27c. Giraudon; 7br, 8r, 9ct, 10bl, 11r & OFC, 14bl, 14ct, 29c. Hulton Getty; 11c, 12c, 15tr, 22l & OBC, 24cl, 31br. Image Select; 9br, 18br, 29br. Images of Africa Photobank; 31tr. Mary Evans Picture Library; 6c, 9tl, 24/25t. NHPA; 4/5t. © Patrick Lorette-Giraudon, Giraudon photographie; 29c. Pix; 2bl, 3b & OFC, 6t, 27tr. Planet Earth Pictures; 2tl, 4/5c, 8tl, 16/17b, 23tr. Rex Features; 30/31ch. South African Library; 9c, 24tl. Telegraph Colour Library; IFC/1, 2tl, 3cb, 12/13t. Werner Forman Archive; 4/5b

Every effort has been made to trace the copyright holders and we apologize in advance for any unintentional omissions.
We would be pleased to insert the appropriate acknowledgment in any subsequent edition of this publication.